T0066300

play the music of
Burt Bacharach

Music Minus One

6033

SUGGESTIONS FOR USING THIS MMO EDITION

WE HAVE TRIED to create a product that will provide you an easy way to learn and perform these compositions with a full ensemble in the comfort of your own home. The following MMO features and techniques will help you maximize the effectiveness of the MMO practice and performance system:

Because it involves a fixed accompaniment performance, there is an inherent lack of flexibility in tempo. We have observed generally accepted tempi, and always in the originally intended key, but some may wish to perform at a different tempo, or to slow down or speed up the accompaniment for practice purposes; or to alter the piece to a more comfortable key. You can purchase from MMO specialized CD players & recorders which allow variable speed while maintaining proper pitch, and vice versa. This is an indispensable tool for the serious musician and you may wish to look into purchasing this useful piece of equipment for full enjoyment of all your MMO editions.

We want to provide you with the most useful practice and performance accompaniments possible. If you have any suggestions for improving the MMO system, please feel free to contact us. You can reach us by e-mail at *info@musicminusone.com*.

Music Minus One

6033

contents

©2009 MMO Music Group, Inc. All rights reserved.
ISBN 1-59615-096-3

ALFIE

Theme from the Paramount Picture ALFIE

Words by Hal David
Music by Burt Bacharach
Arranged by Jim Odrich

Copyright ©1966 (Renewed 1994) by Famous Music LLC
This arrangement Copyright ©2007 by Famous Music LLC
International Copyright Secured. All Rights Reserved.
Used by permission.

WALK ON BY

Lyric by Hal David
Music by Burt Bacharach
Arranged by Jim Odrich

Copyright ©1964 (Renewed) Casa David and New Hidden Valley Music
This arrangement Copyright ©2007 Casa David and New Hidden Valley Music
International Copyright Secured. All Rights Reserved.
Used by permission.

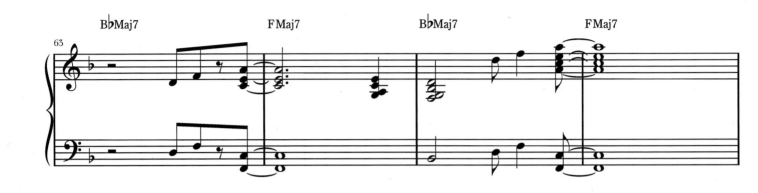

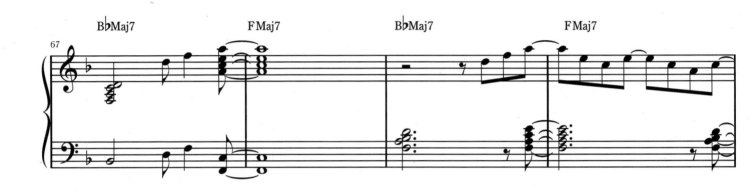

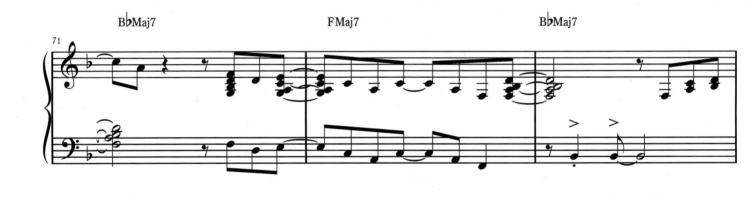

FADE OUT WITH TRACK

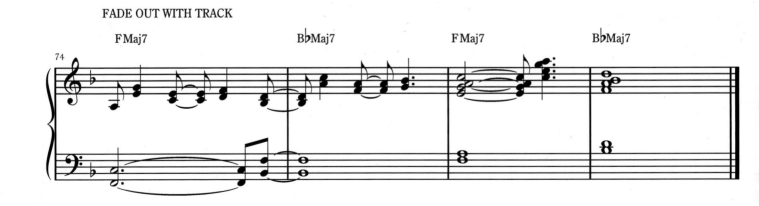

MAGIC MOMENTS

Lyric by Hal David
Music by Burt Bacharach
Arranged by Jim Odrich

Copyright ©1957 (Renewed 1985) by Famous Music LLC and Casa David
This arrangement Copyright ©2007 by Famous Music LLC and Casa David
International Copyright Secured. All Rights Reserved.
Used by permission.

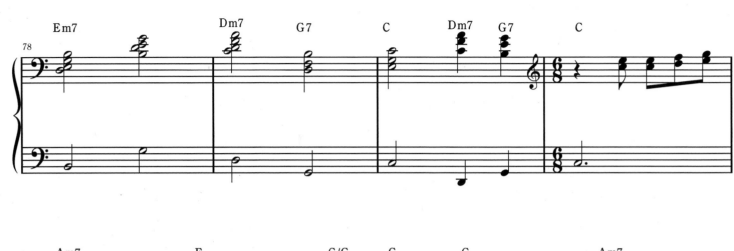

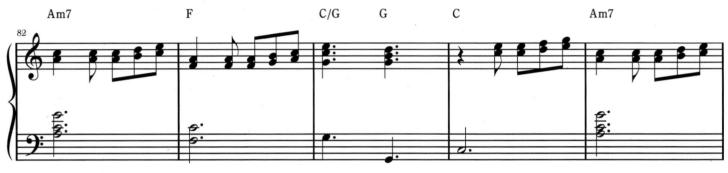

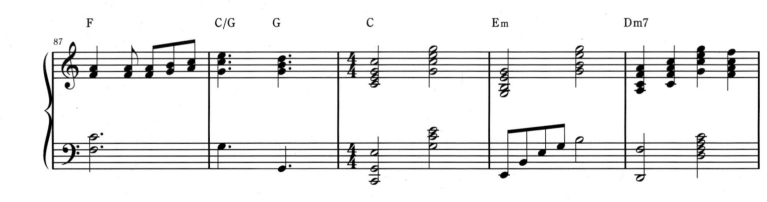

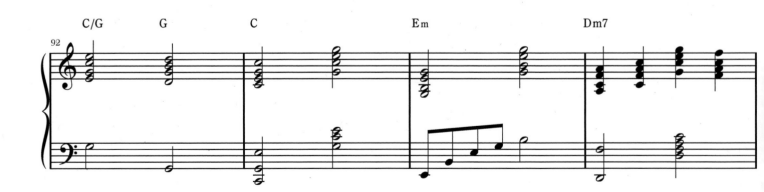

THE WINDOWS OF THE WORLD

Lyric by Hal David
Music by Burt Bacharach
Arranged by Jim Odrich

Copyright ©1967 (Renewed) Casa David and New Hidden Valley Music
This arrangement Copyright ©2007 Casa David and New Hidden Valley Music
International Copyright Secured. All Rights Reserved.
Used by permission.

MMO 6033

BLUE ON BLUE

Lyric by Hal David
Music by Burt Bacharach
Arranged by Jim Odrich

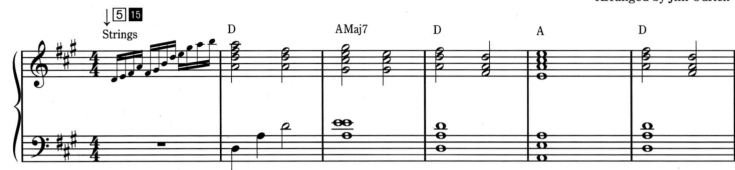

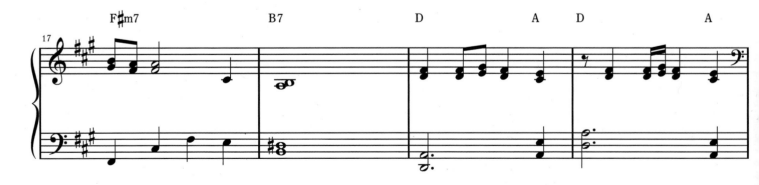

Copyright ©1963 (Renewed) Casa David and New Hidden Valley Music
This arrangement Copyright ©2007 Casa David and New Hidden Valley Music
International Copyright Secured. All Rights Reserved.
Used by permission.

WIVES AND LOVERS (Hey, Little Girl)

from the Paramount Picture WIVES AND LOVERS

Words by Hal David
Music by Burt Bacharach
Arranged by Jim Odrich

Copyright ©1963 (Renewed 1991) by Famous Music LLC
This arrangement Copyright ©2007 by Famous Music LLC
International Copyright Secured. All Rights Reserved.
Used by permission.

26

THIS GUY'S IN LOVE WITH YOU

Lyric by Hal David
Music by Burt Bacharach
Arranged by Jim Odrich

Copyright ©1968 (Renewed) Casa David and New Hidden Valley Music
This arrangement Copyright ©2007 Casa David and New Hidden Valley Music
International Copyright Secured. All Rights Reserved.
Used by permission.

MMO 6033

WHAT THE WORLD NEEDS NOW IS LOVE

Lyric by Hal David
Music by Burt Bacharach
Arranged by Jim Odrich

Copyright ©1965 (Renewed) Casa David and New Hidden Valley Music
This arrangement Copyright ©2007 Casa David and New Hidden Valley Music
International Copyright Secured. All Rights Reserved.
Used by permission.

34

MMO 6033

FADE OUT WITH TRACK TO END

I SAY A LITTLE PRAYER

Lyric by Hal David
Music by Burt Bacharach
Arranged by Jim Odrich

Copyright ©1966 (Renewed) Casa David and New Hidden Valley Music
This arrangement Copyright ©2007 Casa David and New Hidden Valley Music
International Copyright Secured. All Rights Reserved.
Used by permission.

40

MMO 6033

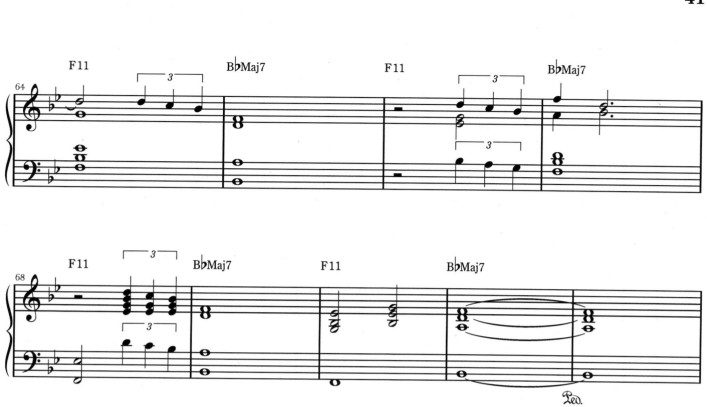

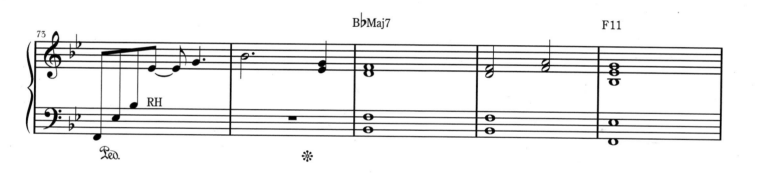

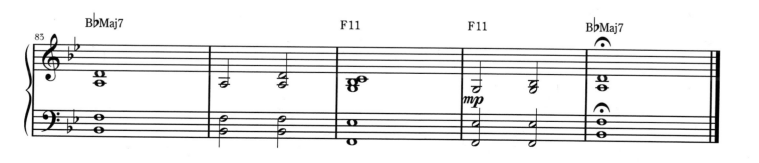

DO YOU KNOW THE WAY TO SAN JOSE

Lyric by Hal David
Music by Burt Bacharach
Arranged by Jim Odrich

Copyright ©1967 (Renewed) Casa David and New Hidden Valley Music
This arrangement Copyright ©2007 Casa David and New Hidden Valley Music
International Copyright Secured. All Rights Reserved.
Used by permission.

46

MMO 6033

FADE OUT GRADUALLY WITH ORCH

MUSIC MINUS ONE
50 Executive Boulevard
Elmsford, New York 10523-1325
800-669-7464 (U.S.)/914-592-1188 (International)

www.musicminusone.com
e-mail: info@musicminusone.com